# Pieces of Me

*poems by*

# Monique Rardin Richardson

*Finishing Line Press*
Georgetown, Kentucky

# Pieces of Me

Copyright © 2024 by Monique Rardin Richardson
ISBN 979-8-88838-773-3 First Edition
All rights reserved under International and Pan-American Copyright Conventions. No part of this book may be reproduced in any manner whatsoever without written permission from the publisher, except in the case of brief quotations embodied in critical articles and reviews.

ACKNOWLEDGMENTS

I have much gratitude to the following publications in which these poems first appeared:

*Viewless Wings Publisher*: "Out-fool the Hands of Time"
Wingless Dreamer Publisher, *Dulce Poetica Anthology*: "We'll Always Have the Moon" and the *Sea or Seashore Anthology*: "When We Collided"
*Quillkeepers Press*: "A Child's Prayer;" "Lips Like Sugar"
Havik: The Las Positas College Journal of Arts & Literature, *We Are Here Anthology*: "Pieces of Me," "Who Should Have Come First," and the *Exomorphosis Anthology:* "Beso Perfecto"

Publisher: Leah Huete de Maines
Editor: Christen Kincaid
Cover Art: Watercolor by Meghana Mitragotri, www.daintlymade.com
Author Photo: Dustin Richardson
Cover Design: Monique Rardin Richardson

Order online: www.finishinglinepress.com
also available on amazon.com

Author inquiries and mail orders:
Finishing Line Press
PO Box 1626
Georgetown, Kentucky 40324
USA

# Contents

Lips Like Sugar ............................................................................ 1
School of Wonder ........................................................................ 2
A Child's Prayer .......................................................................... 3
True Colors .................................................................................. 4
Pieces of Me ................................................................................ 6
Literary Heart ............................................................................. 7
Scattered Pictures ...................................................................... 8
In a field . . . ................................................................................ 9
Creation of Lyrics .................................................................... 10
Beso Perfecto ............................................................................ 11
Now She Knows ....................................................................... 12
When We Collided ................................................................... 13
Chatoyant Eyes ......................................................................... 14
The Seasons of Life ................................................................. 15
She Visits ................................................................................... 16
Radiant Rebel ........................................................................... 17
Abuela Lola ............................................................................... 18
The One ..................................................................................... 19
We'll Always Have the Moon ................................................. 20
Out-fool the Hands of Time ................................................... 21
Under Lock and Key ............................................................... 22
Verdad ....................................................................................... 23
Who's Beside You? .................................................................. 24
Missing a Stanger .................................................................... 25
Who Should Have Come First ............................................... 26
Write, Create, Anything, Something ..................................... 27
The Time Has Come ............................................................... 28
A Single Tear ............................................................................ 29
Carousel .................................................................................... 30
One Step to Happiness ........................................................... 31

*For my son, the young man
who taught me the importance of women using their voices*

**lips like sugar**

the race from the schoolyard to the classroom
in my well-worn canvas sneakers
seemed as far apart as the sweltering Sonoran Desert
to the cool San Francisco breeze

high-pitched screams drowned out faint giggles
and three-year-old girls bumped into one another
like a litter of puppies tripping on their toes
in an attempt to escape the blond hair, blue-eyed
beast

derailed from safety and detained behind the fence
I was captured, single-handed, by—
the kissing bandit

he pressed his purple popsicle-stained lips against mine,
wiped off his sticky, sweet, smiling mouth,
and headed back to the playground, while I stood flushed—

from my very first kiss

## School of Wonder

"The truck can drive by itself, mija."
I didn't believe my Abuela when we
stopped at the top of the hill.

I stood and held the dashboard
peeking out the windshield
of the turquoise 57 Chevy,
when she asked, "Do you want to see?"

I nodded with an impish grin,
then she took her hands off
the steering wheel and the truck moved!

All by itself, it traveled down
the steep mound, while my eyes
popped with curiosity, and my heart
raced as we rolled to the intersection.

I begged her to take control.

She grasped the blue wheel,
and I scooted across the bench seat
"How can it do that, Grandma?"

"It's magic! Es magia Monica. . ."

## A Child's Prayer

I like the way the light of the
stove chases the darkness away
    *Mama, can I stay?*

How grandma has finger clippers
in the drawer by the television
and she files and trims mine so they
aren't sharp like yours
    *Mama, can I stay?*

The Chilean game show host in the
Zenith console speaks Spanish
and makes Grandpa smile and laugh
    *Mama, can I stay?*

It's fun keeping an eye on his cigarette,
making sure when he tips over asleep and the ashes
fall, that I slowly slide it from his fingertips
    *Mama, can I stay?*

Crunchy oatmeal cookies are always on the counter,
next to the cow cookie jar and frosted flakes.
    *Mama, can I stay?*


Abuela lets me cuddle with her before I go to sleep
    *Mama, please,*
        *can I stay?*

**True Colors**

Under the roof of colorless
walls and worry-free wealth
where brand-named cereal was
found in cupboards and consumed
on a marble-topped kitchen counter

Young girls with new pajama sets
lined up in front of a canopy bed,
and its matching furniture, with silver
accents and I was—fitting in

Until the arrival of a boisterous Gold Wing
outside to deliver my forgotten bedding

I cringed to hear my name shouted
from my mother and her boyfriend's
cigarette-cradling mouths over the rev
of an idling engine

I ran out the front door like a brown
hare to retrieve my frayed sleeping bag,
then begged my mother to leave . . . *quickly!*

Up the stairs, I raced back to the bedroom
where I was cornered by a manicured finger
that scolded,

"I saw your filthy parents on that bike.
Mexicans are not allowed here unless
they're trimming my hedges."

Allowed one last phone call, then escorted
to the sidewalk, I waited for—

my mom whose darker skin revealed mine

I listened to laughter stream through
the window of a room I'd spent months in
till she came back in her rusted blue truck

My tears fell, while we polluted
the perfect street, with the flawless
homes by the picturesque beach.

**Pieces of Me**

Questions—the adolescent years
filled with questions.

Not ordinary, angst-ridden,
social engaging, juvenile
thoughts.

No, mine centered on a man.

*Where was he?*
*Did I look like him?*
*Did he love me?*

In the days of seeking Easter eggs
through grape and squash vines,
chased by chickens and geese with
a Siamese cat named Gumdrops,
I was fooled to believe what was in
front of me was truth.

In the search for answers, I found
what I thought was missing in front
of a bar with dirty blond hair,
a swollen red nose and dark circles
under his pale blue eyes.
He resembled a swamp rat
dripping wet from the rain.

And before I could release my words,
he had a demand for me . . .

*I want you to change your last name.*

The question of *who* was replaced
with *why* as I stood on the sidewalk
underneath the dampened moonlit sky,
now—in severed pieces.

**Literary Heart**

It's lovely when a book is so divine
you feel like the characters' lives are on hold
waiting for your return between pages

When bedtime is a favored time
to reunite with crisp cotton sheets
safe in your secluded harbor
alone until one speaks to you
in your quieted thoughts

No one knows where you travel,
except those who share secrets in ink
inviting you onto a literary stage
with friends who reveal hearts
because you're the only one
they choose to confess to

It's a sheer talent to imagine
a story so superb that you want
forever and an ending . . . all at once

**Scattered Pictures**

Mighty raindrops
pummel the admiral blue
umbrella shared by two,
an arm that usually strums a guitar
protects today from the March wind
threatening to wash me away
into the ocean

In a swift move, I'm ushered
into a dimly lit restaurant,
he shakes his jacket like Bogart
then guides me to a table by a fire
where Irish coffee is served to warm
bellies and mirror hearts

*Which view is more pleasing?*

His smile, the iconic bridge,
the other couples, under colorful
canopies on the street below?

I exhale into a palette of perfection.

**In a field...**

full of white, purple, and blue,
I still search for the radiance of amber

A sunny disposition and face toward the light
Why did the wind push too hard, taking you away?

I still look for a glint of gold to carry me home,
but I've lost it—lost you to the wind

All I ever wanted was a dash of yellow
to guide the way, a solid stem for support
and heart-shaped leaves to spiral my waist,
keeping me safe from the hopeless space
we sprouted from

In a field full of flowers, I'd find you—
Because you were the sunflower

**creation of lyrics**

the buzzing neon marquee
on the historic street brought
la magie to the evening air

on a frail bench of distressed wood,
his blue jean covered thigh
pressed against my flowing floral skirt

two lost souls resurrected under a strand
of poorly draped shimmering lights

crowds gathered by the venue, but we
stayed seated in an invisible, isolated
world

music could not stimulate more
then a conversation with a free
spirit and his attentive eyes of green

people faded from the sidewalks
vibrations rattled beveled glass doors
in time with my accelerated heartbeat

and we stayed outside, creating our own
lyrics while the band played on

**Beso Perfecto**
    *(Perfect Kiss)*

The city street corner, painted
in scarlet from the neon signs
and traffic light, bounced off
the wet pavement—while my hand
was held in the warmth of a man
who knew how to free a body
and young mind of pain

When emerald echoed art
on the asphalt, my heel stepped
off the curb, suspended in flight,
until I was pulled back to the sidewalk
and turned into a heated East Coast
embrace, and for the first time,
met with his sultry, soft lips

I don't know how many times
the colors danced in the open air
before our lips parted, but it was
the best unexpected moment
devoured from his confidence
and my desire to be his desired

**Now She Knows**

She offered to be a temporary
placeholder until true love was found

Tongue-tied when near her,
he shared his private thoughts in a song
each one more revealing than the last

"Yes," he said, "But never temporary."

The ethereal blue in her heart
turned passionate pink on her cheeks
as requited lyrics danced in her head

No longer did she listen with a hopeful heart.

**When We Collided**

You, the free-flowing water
      fierce and unattainable

Me, the fragile sandcastle
      admiring from a distance

slow movements inch closer,
      then slide away,
closer,
      then resistance

Enveloped by the traveling tide,
the weakened structure succumbs to the water,
and there's no more—
      all's dissolved into one

The waves are breathtaking,
unaware of their beauty and power
      They can't stop,
           can't control,
                can't change

It just is . . .

**chatoyant eyes**

sang to me of a love not had,
no one saw his pain, so I listened
for years and a day more, I listened

he tore poems from my heart
made me smile in the dark
'til I left a message with the rain
I'd no longer meet and play—but I did

I danced in his somber
found the rainbow in his cloud
thought the sea one day might rise
to give back stolen sleep
or release the blanket cast in grey
but the day never came
so I miss

I offer a kiss to the wind
and I miss

**The Seasons of Life**

He reached for my hand
when showers caressed
the canary yellow roses
and the rust-chested robin serenaded
during a misty Sunday stroll

He laced his rugged fingers with mine
as we walked under the luminary light
palms slippery from humidity or . . .
*was his heart beating fast, too?*

He held on tight to my persistent heart
when the leaves turned to butterscotch
and slipped away from the lonely
branch, leaving a brave one behind

Our fingers remained intertwined
through the brittle chill in the air
and the darkened days that soon followed

Decades of derailing dreams—
and now my hand grips this ceramic fountain pen,

to feel something

**She visits**

in my dreams
where she's safe

the wind tickles
her flawless skin
and golden ringlets
brush her shoulders
as wheat sways
in the Kansas wind

She sits in grains
of caramel-colored sand
sweeping it with perfect
pink fingertips

A never seen face
but a heartbeat
in rhythm with mine

She slipped from my body
without warning

A body that still sheds tears
from a bond only we know existed

She waits . . .
for a day that will never come

## Radiant Rebel

When she rises
from darkness,
she awakens me
painting brilliant
colors across the sky
Picasso's dream seen
through opened eyes

The ethereal glow
energizes like a sweet
orange of summer,
waiting to be picked
from dewy limbs
I bask in her beauty
for tomorrow—

she may not be seen

**Abuela Lola**

She said, "Take it,"
as she pushed the cotton fabric
rolled in her tiny arms and hands
to my chest

"You will be left with nothing,
I don't want you to have nothing.
Please, take it, Mija."

She tried to lift it within my reach
with her aged angelic body,
not ready for the end

If the quilt were to unravel
my grandmother would disappear
which she was doing day by excruciating,
*I don't want to think about it*—day

I reassured her I didn't need anything
but her memory tucked in my mind and heart,
although I took it . . .

I relieved her of its weight and pressed it to my lap,
petting it as if it breathed

Today, I'm reminded of women
with strong, creative hands
as I bury myself in the ivory quilt
embroidered with cardinal roses,
emerald vines, and her touch.

Knowing who I am and what I do,
I learned from her—and I rest

**the one**

you're the book marker of my life
the one who slipped into chapters
leaving stains on the pages
and tears in my eyes

the one who darkened my days
and gave me sunny skies

how do I say goodbye?

**We'll Always Have the Moon**

It's been years
but still, I feel her gaze

When I turn to find my lost friend
in the shadows, I see golden waves rush by
like a mermaid heading back to sea
or a wood nymph dashing through
a sultry forbidden forest

She teases, sending a spark of a smile
as bright as a shooting star

My wishful dream watches
with eyes of emerald green

She always said, "I was the wind beneath her wings,"
but she's an angel now waking me by moonlight

We talk under a galaxy of blue,
then she disappears, and I patiently wait
for another milky pearl in the night
to unveil her next visit

**Out-fool the Hands of Time**

If I whisper, maybe it will not hear
Its secondhand will quit ticking forward
The ones I love won't fade and disappear
I'll cherish your gift now; you have my word

I want my memories shared to exist
in more than my lonely and aging mind
All the talks not had and words of love missed
For some, moments and stars—never align

I refuse to be the sole keeper; please stay
Beat the dreaded hands of time together
So we can share another walk one day
Leave our thoughts light as a fallen feather

Speak quietly so the clock we can fool
Time can be lovely, but when lost—so cruel

**under lock and key**

ever since you
passed
I feel something is
missing
and if I look hard
enough—

I will find you

in the supermercado
racing down the aisle
or on the street,
walking in the sunshine
without a care

but no matter how hard
I stare at a stranger,
it will not create you

*mi vez en la vida*
who I can only find—

in my heart

## Verdad

I cried from a portrayal
of my life shown on screen.

The struggle of being half
in a world that expects whole.

I don't have the right skin,
last name, or tongue.

But I am—a Mexican.

As authentic on the inside
as others on the outside.

My memories tell me so.

**Who's Beside You?**

Who holds your hand
when you sit down to write
and your body reminds your heart
it still cries?

Who stops the nightmares
that come to claim a victim
while you scribe into the dark
and isolated night?

Who softly grips your hand,
helping you shed demons
and encourages you to wait
for daybreak?

Who walks the path of the past,
and stops the flow of tears that find you,
though you've kept them hidden for years?

Who teaches you what to hold onto
and what to erase?

I don't know—maybe that's why I scribble in ink.

**Missing a Stranger**

I miss the whos and whats in life,
I miss what I don't know.
The sturdy knee and lap to climb,
a chart measuring how one grows.

The handsome man with whiskers,
a resemblance to this face, a tiara
for my head, or being donned in blue
tulle and lace.

Carried to bed, tucked in cozy
with him by my side, stories read aloud,
a strong male presence as a guide.

*Isn't this what fathers do?*

No longer a child, a woman now
still in need of the love he couldn't show.

## Who Should Have Come First

In an enchanting dark room, we stood surrounded
by nothing but a view of one another
and a history spanning decades

To the left, an ex-lover trying to be a friend
He declared to be in my life until his last breath
but could never be reached when I needed his voice
A man who roamed the earth like the wind,
detached from promises, even ones made to himself

To the right, a dreamer, so full of passion,
he couldn't stay connected because of the "fantasy"
affair taking place in his self-made Garden of Eden
He feared himself if the happiness dissolved,
and me, since he believed he was not deserving

Straight ahead in the distance, a mirror
I pushed the silhouette to the left and watched him
scatter into pieces and fly away like the seeds
of a dandelion finding a new place
to consume its inner beauty

My hand rested on the heartbeat of the figure
on the right, watched him crumble like a sandcastle
slipping away with the force of waves on land

and I awoke . . . and stepped towards myself

## Write, Create, Anything, Something

I don't know what I want to *write* today.
But my pencil wants to skate along the blank page,
leaving grooves within the paper
like blades etching tracks on winter ice.
A mark someone was there.

I want to create—construct—compose.

Thoughts scatter through my mind in search of a muse who's decided
to play a game of hide and seek within.

Are these feelings a sign of boredom?
Inner peace?
Lack of sincere interest?
Or something else?

I don't want to do *anything*.
But I need to do *something*.
I'm restless and trapped by disorganized thoughts,
with the freedom to do as I choose with unpenciled time,
and I choose this . . .

To wrestle with an ideation I can't convert into words
on a solid page of white.

Maybe I'll take a walk.

**the time has come**

free me of the overgrowth
of memories and heartbreak
taking place within, so light
can break through and sprout
a new way of living and learning

gift me patience
to wade out of the darkness
and examine the ocean waves
until morning, when the tide
reveals what's underneath
the turbulent sea

let me breathe in, listen to the wind
tell stories of those before me
I'll hear them if I open my mind's window
and allow the breeze of words to travel
into silence and strip my heart
of what I can't see in myself,
but am now ready to release

## A Single Tear

"Do you love me?"
The words escaped her heart-shaped lips
echoed off the moonlit walls of solitude
and a single tear slipped from her eye
landing on her sapphire silk robe
now stained and robbed of its perfection

The night's end promised a clarity unfound
even though sunbeams cavorted across the tiled sink
and maple leaves brushed the windowsill, waving hello,
she sat at the distressed table made for one
writing the same question in her journal
until gently closing the unanswered pages

Hot water beat down on her rosy skin
while a lifetime of mistakes and bad decisions
projected into her freshly lathered head, and the question
flashed like a headline, forcing her to ask once more,

"Do you love me?"

She stared intently into the mirror,
past the flaws internally tattooed on the glass
and a smile materialized at what she discovered
nestled in the steam.

No longer requiring a masculine voice,
her index finger etched across the reflection.

"Yes, I do."

**Carousel**

Words—floating Oxford
blue ink patterns encompass
every thought until spilled onto
barren paper for spectators to see

Some rise like a decadent carved
mahogany horse, galloping round
in search of the golden ring
while others speak of rain clouds
taunting my sunshine with a promise
to fade away when shared

I sit before others with a reluctant smile
on my painted face, while words
reappear whispering,

*"Step back, watch life from a distance,*
*keep the dream in your heart*
*knowing the music may pause,*
*but it will never end.*
*Keep these images to yourself,*
*my sensitive friend."*

Yet I continue writing, letting intimate
thoughts drizzle onto the pages, hoping
others will understand
my carousel of emotions

**One Step to Happiness**

And the day came—
when she looked in her
rearview mirror
on a long drive
and saw her history
descend farther
and farther out of sight
and she felt calm,
safe, and ready
to say goodbye—
not only to the past
but the version of herself
she no longer was—

and no longer
wanted to be.

**With Thanks**

I have to start by thanking my husband and son for continuously being the beacon of my creativity. Whenever I stumble or waver off course, you are both there to guide me back to my passion and forever remind me who I am and what I love to do. Thank you for your love and support. I'd be lost without you.

To my poetry group (past and present participants), who are there month after month to help me hone my work with patience and the utmost care, I'm a stronger writer because of each of you. I carry you all with me with every poem I write.

I want to thank Meghana for sharing her extraordinary talent in creating the perfect watercolor portrait of Pieces of Me—a piece of art I'll treasure.

To all of my family and friends, you made me who I am. Please know that whether near or far, you remain in my heart.

And to all those who need to hear this—you are already complete and whole, just as you are.

**Monique Rardin Richardson** found the joy of reading early in life while snuggled in bed as a child and began writing poetry and short stories in middle school to help her process life. She didn't realize until much later that being a writer and photographer was an unfulfilled dream. With an open mind and willing heart, she realized there was still time to start delving into her almost forgotten passions, photography and writing, and is now the author of *Despina the Anti-Cupid*, *The Unlikely Dreamcatcher*, and an award-winning memoir written about a lifelong friend with addictions, titled *When Then Became Now* and has had several poems published in anthologies and journals.

As a half-Mexican woman, Monique's cultural roots are deeply embedded in her poetry and stories. She weaves her heritage into her work, hoping that it resonates with others who share a similar background. For years, she kept her thoughts and work private and to herself. However, as she grows older, she's learning to tend to her voice and speak it like the strong people of all ages she admires today.

Monique is from Northern California and is a member of the California Writer's Club, Dublin Arts Collective, and Pleasanton Art League, with award-winning photos in the United States galleries, including the de Young Museum's 2023 Open Show in San Francisco, CA.

Milton Keynes UK
Ingram Content Group UK Ltd.
UKHW040255291024
450401UK00006B/49